Chelsea s
from its e

John Bignell has lived in Chelsea for more than
forty years and has been a professional
photographer for most of that time. His early work
covered a wide range – babies to photojournalism,
industry to the theatre. His work has appeared in
such magazines as *Paris Match*, *Life* and Norman
Hall's prestigious magazine *Photography*. In recent
years, he has concentrated more on his first love,
art, a move that has brought him into contact with
artists, many of them closely associated with
Chelsea.

to Catherine

Chelsea seen

from its earliest days

A collection of photographs
and engravings selected
by John Bignell

CONTENTS

© *John Bignell 1978 and 1987*
First published in Great Britain 1978
Revised and enlarged edition 1987
First paperback edition 1992
Reprinted 1994

ISBN 0 7090 4976 5

Robert Hale Limited
Clerkenwell House
Clerkenwell Green
London EC1R 0HT

Printed in Great Britain by
St Edmundsbury Press Limited
Bury St Edmunds, Suffolk and
bound by WBC Bookbinders Limited.

Aldin's Wharf, c.1870.

Coal and other bulk goods were brought by barge to be unloaded at the numerous wharves on the Chelsea bank.

Introduction

It could be said that this book was first conceived fifteen or twenty years ago when I came across in the Chelsea library a small collection of nineteenth century photographs by a man called James Hedderley. They covered a period of some fifteen years from about 1860 to 1875 and, apart from their photographic quality, were obviously of considerable interest to anyone with a feeling for local history.

Jim Barnard, editor of the local paper—then still known as the "West London Press"—asked me to make copies of the Hedderley photographs for a series he was running under the heading "This Was Chelsea." There were only about twenty photographs in good enough condition and, although there seemed to be a nucleus here, it was not until much more material had been accumulated from various sources that a book of this size could be contemplated.

I came to live in Chelsea in the early part of the war and, since about 1950, have worked as a photographer in and around this part of London. It is impossible to live in the place for nearly forty years without developing an addiction for it, and trying to discover why—like those other small bits of large cities, Montmartre, Greenwich Village and so on—it is so well-known all over the world. Even the adjective 'Chelsean' has a distinctive, though difficult to define, meaning.

It has, of course, a long and interesting history, and is chiefly associated with its many distinguished residents from King Henry the Eighth, Thomas More, Nell Gwynne, and a whole host of artists and men of letters, throughout the centuries to the present day. But that is only part of its charm which, indeed, could be matched by many other parts of London. There *is* something special about Chelsea.

Little is known about Hedderley himself except that he was a signwriter in old Duke Street in the 1860's. He moved to Riley Street in World's End when the whole area of small shops and wharves between the church and Battersea Bridge were due for demolition to make way for the western extension of Cheyne Walk. Nearly all the photographs that have survived were taken within a few hundred yards of that heart of old Chelsea that stretched from the Old Swan pub to Chelsea Reach. In what appears to be quite a short period of time—the exact dates of his photographs are not known—he made a remarkable record of a lost era. The little village that Turner, Carlyle, Whistler and Greaves knew so well was largely swept away by the civic zeal for improvement in the 1870's. Almost as if in retribution for that unique bit of Dickensian London being so 'improved' it was wiped out again—including the Old Church this time—by a particularly vicious Goering bomb in April 1941. Miraculously the church was re-built fifteen years later. But keen Chelsea gardeners commandeered the site of Lombard Terrace (formerly Duke Street) and it eventually became formalised into the present sunken Roper's garden, named after Thomas More's son-in-law.

It gives one an eerie sense of the reality of time and the impact of modern developments to sit in that small but pleasant oasis, hearing the muffled roar of the juggernauts on the adjacent embankment road, while being reminded of the bustling little Victorian village centre and the busy wharves that once covered that very spot.

Hedderley even took his cumbersome 10" x 12" view camera and tripod to the top of the church tower to obtain what must be one of the finest panoramas of any London suburb more than a hundred years ago. Having myself negotiated those narrow spiralling steps to the same viewpoint more recently, albeit with only a small modern camera to encumber me, I can testify to his commendable enterprise and physical stamina.

Thea Holme in her book on Chelsea, published during the 'swinging Chelsea' period, relates a nice story about a young foreign visitor who stopped her in Cheyne Walk to ask where was "the 'eart of Chelsea?" He was, of course, looking for the King's Road and it's high-decibel boutiques and was nonplussed when she pointed out that he was in fact standing in the historical manor of Henry the Eighth, Thomas More, Nell Gwynne and the rest. She was referring to that earlier period when Chelsea really *was* the Village of Palaces. Most of the palaces had already disappeared by the second half of the

These two young ladies in the fashion of the 1860s are standing by the Hans Sloane memorial outside Chelsea Old Church. Surprisingly it survived the almost total destruction of the building in 1941. See p. 73.

nineteenth century when enterprising photographers like Hedderley started to set up their mahogany and brass contraptions in the streets to record the contemporary scene. In those days of slow emulsions and long exposures any passer-by had to stand still for several seconds in order to achieve a kind of immortality that, in previous generations, would have required many hours of static posing for an artist to translate the scene in his own subjective style to the canvas. Or, indeed, for a writer to describe it even more subjectively on paper.

The impact and immediacy of these early photographs of domestic and street scenes is now generally recognised, hence their universal appeal. The viewer can relate directly with what appears in the photographic print without needing any artistic education. When some Victorians tried to imitate fashionable academic art by setting up posed groups in the studio or tried to compose sentimental studies of nature, they could never compete with an even moderately competent painter. Faster emulsions and the instantaneous shutter soon changed all that.

Down to earth photographers, like Hedderley, ignored the child who ran across the field of view to leave a ghostly shadow on his plate. He made his prints, warts and all, to delight us with un-retouched and unsentimentalised scenes of his day. Almost all the pictures in this book dated prior to about 1878 are by him, unless otherwise attributed. The later 19th century and early 20th century ones are from various sources and mostly by unknown photographers. The modern (post-war) illustrations are all selected from my own negative files to bring the kaleidoscopic changes in this smallest of London's boroughs up to the present day.

In a nostalgic exercise such as this one must be careful not to view the past with too rose-coloured a pair of spectacles. Many of the changes have been for the good. But few would now dispute that the amalgamation of Chelsea some dozen years ago with the much larger Royal Borough of Kensington has accelerated a process that was already beginning. The individuality of Chelsea as a village has virtually disappeared.

Like a country pub that used to charm one with its good ale and good company Chelsea has, perhaps, been too successful for most of its older inhabitants who knew it as it was a generation or more ago. Yet—who knows?—there may also be many who, discovering it for the first time as it is to-day, will look back with nostalgia at those 'swinging sixties'—and even the era of punk!

Beaufort Street
1978

Right: A photograph taken through the clock face in 1957 during the rebuilding of Chelsea Old Church, looking across the river Thames to the Battersea side.

Introduction to new edition

Scarcely ten years on and, indeed, the punks are almost gone. The Chelsea Scene changes fast. The Sloane Rangers came and went, but the yuppies are, as always, very much with us.

But, gratifyingly, *Chelsea Seen* soon went out of print. With a continuing steady demand apparent, an enlarged and updated edition seemed desirable if suitable material were available. Nineteenth-century photographs of the quality and topographical interest of Hedderley's are rare.

By lucky chance in 1983 I moved a couple of hundred yards westward from Beaufort Street into the peaceful oasis of the Moravian Close. It is perhaps the most significant two acres, historically speaking, in the whole of Chelsea being intimately linked to the very earliest days some 450 years ago when the small rural village west of London began to develop into the 'Village of Palaces'.

Thomas More may not have been the first Chelsea commuter, but he *was* the Chancellor of England and, then, on very good terms with King Henry. So, when he bought land and built a Great House here in 1523, he certainly gave a boost to the already known desirable attractions of the area up-wind from the city smells and up-river from the inevitable pollutions.

I am writing this in the cottage built in 1753 by the Moravians (refugees from religious persecution) upon the foundations of More's stables and overlooking what had for two centuries been the stableyard, and which since then has been the Moravian burial ground.

Inevitably, it seems, any expansion of this book has to look backward to its earliest days of semi-rural glory with the intellectual and artistic attractions that came with its élite immigrants. And this, of course, was long before the age of photography.

But Kip's View on pp. 156-7 gives the sort of panoramic view of the western half of Chelsea that any photographer today would need the assistance of a helicopter to equal.

The Manse, Moravian Close
1987

Joe McCulloch in 1951. He looked and behaved so much like the typical "Chelsea Artist" of the period that he actually became known as the "last of the Bohemians". He taught for many years at St Martin's School of Art and lived in Garden studios, Manresa Road.

Very Important People

Top: Councillors and others at the annual Oak Apple Day parade of pensioners at the Royal Hospital, c.1956.
Below: "The Earl and Lady Cadogan at home, 1897." So runs the caption to this photograph when the then Earl was Governor General in Dublin. The present Earl is his grandson.

Little People

Top: In Marlborough Street (now Draycott Avenue), c.1900.
Below: Small art lovers selling pictures outside the Chelsea swimming baths, 1955.

Top left: A scene in Radnor Walk recorded c.1930 by George Buchanan from the entrance to his premises where he built hand-pushed milk floats, now the Chelsea Pottery.

Bottom left: This pavement artist displayed his wares for many years in King's Road against the railings of Paultons Square. Note the Chelsea A.R.P. (Air Raid Precautions) exhortation to bring gas masks for inspection.

Right: Sir Lewis Casson and Dame Sybil Thorndike after recording their vote at the 1964 general election.

Below: Karl Marx and family with Frederick Engels. When the family first came to England in 1849 they lived for several months at 4 Anderson Street, Chelsea. In the front row are Jenny, Eleanor and Laura.

Old houses in Sloane Square demolished 1892.

Right: Sloane Square. In the foreground, the fountain designed by Gilbert Ledward, R.A. and erected in 1953 as a gift from the Royal Academy to the Borough of Chelsea.
The picture was taken from the roof of Peter Jones store during the handing over ceremony.

At the top of the photograph is the Royal Court Theatre, built in 1888 by Bertie Crewe on the site of an earlier theatre.

The Royal Court Theatre has a long and distinguished history of innovation, starting with the administration of Harvey Granville-Barker and J. E. Vedrenne who took over in 1904 and produced eleven plays by George Bernard Shaw, six of them for the first time, so establishing him as the leading playwright of his generation. Among their other artistic successes were Galsworthy's *The Silver Box* and Granville-Barker's own play, *The Voysey Inheritance*.

Above: An early poster.

Left: Sloane Square, c. 1900.

The Royal Court became a cinema in 1935, only re-opening as a theatre, after extensive restoration following severe bomb damage, in 1952. Its second golden age came about four years later when George Devine and his English Stage Company bought it. His third production, John Osborne's *Look Back In Anger*, with Alan Bates and Mary Ure, set the tone for what was to follow. In a few years Devine consolidated his reputation for launching young dramatists, among them Harold Pinter, Arnold Wesker and Samuel Beckett.

Above: The Aldermaston marchers approaching Sloane Square, Easter, 1960.

Left: Holy Trinity Church, c. 1903. It was built by J. Sedding in 1890
to replace the one designed by James Savage in 1830.

Knightsbridge, looking towards
Hyde Park Corner, c. 1905.
The Hyde Park Hotel dominates
the northern side as it does today.
It was built in 1882
as Hyde Park Court, a block of flats
for gentlemen, on the site
of The Fox and Bull,
one of Knightbridge's most historic
taverns which boasted a sign painted
by Sir Joshua Reynolds.
In 1904 the flats were partly
destroyed by fire, re-built and opened
as an hotel. In those days
it had 300 rooms, each with bathroom
and lavatory, and luxury of luxuries,
electric light throughout.
Opposite the hotel is Harvey Nichols
occupying part of the old
Spring Gardens. They included
a World's End tavern (equally
as disreputable as the Chelsea one)
where Samuel Pepys, ever an
enthusiastic reveller, "ate a mess of
cream, was merry and tarried late".

Brompton Oratory is named after the Oratory founded by St Philip Neri in Rome in 1578 and brought to England by Cardinal Newman in 1848. Herbert Gribble won the competition held in 1878 to decide the architect, his ornate Italian designs best expressing the atmosphere of devotion required for a Roman Catholic church at that time. The Church was opened in 1884 though the facade and dome were not completed until 1897. The interior is especially notable for the unusually wide nave (52 feet). The Renaissance altar in the Lady chapel came from Brescia and the series of marble statues of the apostles, made by G. Mazzioli between 1680 and 1685, from Siena Cathedral.

A cab rank in Brompton Road with the Oratory rising behind it.

King's Road, looking east from a roof on the corner of Oakley Street, c. 1959,
Chelsea Palace was pulled down in the 1960's.

King's Road, looking west from the roof of Peter Jones, 1953. The bank building with Clock Tower has since been replaced by a western extension of the department store.

The annual May Day Festival at the College, a custom started by John Ruskin in 1881. One girl was elected as Queen of the May, her prize a present from the great man. She then chose some of her friends to receive signed copies of Ruskin's books.

Whiteland's College

Ladies' education came to Chelsea in 1772 when the Reverend John Jenkins opened his school for "Female Education and Christian Fortitude under Affliction". History doesn't relate what the afflictions were but the establishment must have thrived for it continued in one form or another until the 1930's when the building came down to make way for the block of flats, Whiteland's Court, that stands there today. In 1842, when bought by the National Society for the Training of School-mistresses, it formally became Whiteland's Training College.

Whiteland's College from the back. The May Day ceremonies took place on the lawns behind the building.

Whiteland's College from King's Road.

Looking back at Chelsea over the span of a not very long life reveals some dramatic changes. There are people alive today who can remember the King's Road as a thoroughfare for horse buses, a predominantly residential street served by friendly neighbourhood shops providing the basic necessities of life. Rapid development began around the turn of the century and continued unabated until the first World War brought it to a temporary halt. Note in the following pages how these changes affected a few key points.

Right: The site of the old Town Hall, completed in 1906, c. 1890.
Below: As it is today.

Next page: The Six Bells shortly after it was built in 1901.

Queen Victoria's Diamond Jubilee 1897—The Conservative Club.

The Old Chelsea Vestry Hall decorated for the 1897 Jubilee. The new Town Hall was built in 1906.

King's Parade, a once elegant terrace pulled down in the late 1950's to make way for Chelsea College and the Fire Stat

"The Last Days of Garden Studios"
They were immediately behind the corner house
in the centre of the large photograph.

Next page: Chelsea students collecting for Thalidomide victims in King's Road, c. 1962.

The Old Burial Ground, opposite the Six Bells Tavern, was given to the parish by Sir Hans Sloane and consecrated by the Bishop of London in 1736. Beyond is the old workhouse, which continued in the same use until the repeal of the Poor Laws in 1947.

Sydney Street, c.1910. The Board of Guardians building is on the left and the Chelsea Palace on the right-hand corner with King's Road.

In 1935 Roy Alderson, the well-known muralist and coup de l'oeil specialist took over Ada Peters' antique shop at no. 144 King's Road. With his father he ran it for nearly twenty years under the pseudonym of Horace Walpole. The old taxi, decorated in Roy's inimitable style, was as much a tourist attraction as a business vehicle during the early fifties when the road displayed an air of gentle eccentricity rather than the boutique bedlam it was so soon to become.

For a brief period before the storm, no. 144 was an early example of the coffee-bar era before the lease was finally sold to a Chinese restaurateur. Within months, it seemed, Mary Quant invaded the neighbouring corner of Markham Square – and she conquered!

Apart from the obvious changes in transport and fashion styles there was little visible difference in the quiet, unhurried atmosphere of streets in the first fifty years of this century.

With few exceptions the shops and public buildings, built mostly in the decades before the first World War, were respectable but undistinguished, and with little relationship to one another.

King's Road, c.1905. Looking west from Walpole & Anderson Street.

The north side of King's Road between Sydney Street and Manor Street.

Top left: The Wilkinson Sword factory, pulled down in 1902 to make way for Chelsea Palace *(far left)*.
Left: The residential and shopping development which replaced the Palace in the late 1960's.
Above: The short terrace next to the Wilkinson Sword factory, c. 1890.
Below: The Post Office and bank building on the same site in 1978.

Above: A typical Edwardian drawing-room, c. 1910, probably No. 4, The Vale.

Above: One of four or five substantial houses, set in their own grounds, that stood in The Vale during the 19th century. Among the famous residents of the leafy cul-de-sac were William and Evelyn de Morgan who lived at No. 1 for twenty-two years and Whistler who occupied No. 2 from 1886 to 1890. When he moved to 21 Cheyne Walk, the house was taken over by Charles Ricketts and Charles Shannon who set up The Vale Press there.

Right: The Vale, 1978.

Glebe Place, c. 1900. The street cuts
through the domain of the original
Chelsea Rectory which consisted in 1650
of a parsonage house with 20 acres of glebe
valued at £60 (glebe, from the Latin gleba
meaning turf, soil or ground,
was applied in English specifically to land
belonging to the church). It also provided
a back way to Shrewsbury House.
It was only in 1870 that the Chelsea
Rectory Act enabled the kitchen garden
to be leased for building. The
terraces in Glebe Place were then built
and also the studios shown in the photograph.
The most famous occupant, the sculptor
Derwent Wood, worked in the 'removals'
building after it was replaced with the
new studios in 1923.
The origins of the white cottage,
thought to be the oldest building standing
in Chelsea, are obscure though the widely
held view that it was an entrance lodge
to Shrewsbury House is probably false.
Since 1928 it has been the home of the
Chelsea Open Air Nursery School.

Above: Dr Lee's surgery on the corner of King's Road and Beaufort Street,
c. 1890. The surgery was demolished c. 1903 and replaced with shops and flats *(below)*.

The north side of King's Road, facing Paulton Square, c. 1895 *(above)* and in 1977 *(below)*.

Dr Phené—Eccentric of Oakley Street

The house in Oakley Street, popularly known as 'gingerbread Castle',
created by Dr John Samuel Phené, one of the most celebrated Chelsea characters
during Victorian and Edwardian times. That his taste was not always so opulent
is proved by his designs for part of the rest of Oakley Street
and the classical Margaretta Terrace, named after his bride, Margaretta Forsyth.

He also planted these streets with trees, an innovation that was rapidly copied
by the Prince Consort outside the new Victoria and Albert Museum.

The Chateau, started in 1901 and never completed, was a reconstruction
of the Phené ancestral home at Savenay on the banks of the Loire, hence the stone carving
over the door, "Renaissance du Chateau de Savenay". Dr Phené, by then a recluse,
never moved into his Chateau, living across the street in No. 32 until his death in 1912.
It was demolished c. 1917.

Dr Phené's other interests of archaeology and anthropology were reflected
in the garden of the Chateau, which pre-dated the house.
There he would sit musing hour after hour, protected from interlopers
by a lock of his own design and surrounded by hideous statues in the classical style.

The nineteenth century gardener, Mr Shailer, grew lavender and the first moss rose here.

Dr Phené later dug up a Roman skull and discovered
a section of the underground passage between the river and Shrewsbury House,
which was built on part of King Henry VIII's Manor of Chelsea.

The photographs on these two pages were taken by R. A. Inglis before World War I.

For one brash outrageous decade London swung and nowhere more vigorously than the King's Road which became the symbol of everything frothy, fashionable and fun. The explosion was triggered by the meeting of the like minds of Alexander Plunket-Greene, proprietor of the first Chelsea set coffee bar on the corner of Markham Square, and a young fashion graduate, Mary Quant, who lived in a bedsit in Oakley Street. Together they opened Bazaar, setting in motion a chain of events that changed Chelsea irrevocably for residents and visitors alike.

In a few short months King's Road, then a straggling street of small useful shops, became a boutique owner's paradise. The historic Thomas Crapper, of water closet fame, gave way to Skin. Brightly painted signs with names like Granny Takes a Trip and Hung on You, sprung up all over, specialists in instant fashion sold with the help of non-stop high decibel pop.

On Saturday afternoons the beautiful and the rich paraded, wearing less and less costing more and more. They dropped into the Chelsea Potter for a drink, ate in Le Reve, Au Pere Nico, Alvaro's, danced in Raffles, Angelique, the Club del'Arethusa, bought modish junk in the Chelsea Antique Market. Among them Michael Caine, David Bailey, Terence Stamp, Vidal Sassoon, David Hemmings . . . the list goes on and on.

Left: The New Jazz Club, set up in the Six Bells in the 1950's.

Below: People on parade and sitting outside the Picasso Cafe.
Life may have seemed like one long game but it wasn't:
not anyway for Claudie Danniel Delbarre (with the blonde curls
in the centre photograph), an 18 year old French au pair girl
who was murdered in her Walpole Street bedsitter
the weekend this photograph was taken in September, 1967.

In King's Road anything goes—but what exactly?

Let's twist again at a local youth club.

The oldest and grandest houses in Cheyne Walk are the low numbers, those between what is now Royal Hospital Road and Oakley Street. In the early 19th century the effect was of a Dutch canal, a mood that lasted until the 1870's when the Embankment, stopped at the Royal Hospital in 1848 due to lack of funds, was finally completed.

The New Manor of Chelsea (on the site of Nos. 19-26) was originally owned by Henry VIII. It was the death place of his fourth wife, Anne of Cleves, and the childhood home of his daughter, the future Queen Elizabeth I. In the 18th century it was bought by Sir Hans Sloane who lived there and also used it to house his famous collection, later the nucleus of the British Museum. His letting off of land to the east of the Manor in 1717 triggered the first building.

In such an imposing street, it is not surprising to find a colourful range of inhabitants. George Eliot died in No. 4 in 1908 while No. 5 was the home of a mean but fashionable jeweller, James Nield, who became an ardent campaigner for prison reform. His son, inheriting his frugality but not his charity, amassed a fortune of £500,000 which he left to Queen Victoria on his death in 1852, providing her with some much needed private wealth. Next door, in the much larger No. 6, Dr Dominicetti, a Venetian aristocrat, opened the first Fumigatory Steam Baths in 1765, numbering the Duke of York among his early patrons. After he fled, hopelessly in debt, in 1782, the house was turned into a school, run by the Reverend Weeden Butler.

One of the most beautiful houses is No. 16, built in 1719 by John Witt, and variously known as Queen's House and Tudor House. It is chiefly associated with Dante Gabriel Rossetti who took it over in 1862 at an annual rent of £110. At first he shared it with George Meredith, Charles Algernon Swinburne and his brother, William, but they soon left him in sole possession. Believing, wrongly, in the house's royal origins, Rossetti filled it with a lavish mixture of antiques, many of them bought in junk shops across the river, and the garden with a noisy menagerie that included a white bull that dug up the lawn, a kangaroo that murdered its mother, a racoon that murdered the kangaroo and a peacock that died under the sofa. In the early years Rossetti loved entertaining but the house that had been his showpiece gradually became his prison as hypochondria and chloral-induced paranoia took hold of him. Nevertheless both he and Swinburne did much of their best work here.

The Embankment now runs to the extreme right of the picture with Embankment Gardens replacing the boats.

Left: Goldings Pier Hotel seen from Cadogan Pier. The hotel was opened in 1844,
a crescent-shaped Victorian pub with a vaguely nautical air.
It survived for over a century until the site was sold
together with the Blue Cockatoo and Thurston's Billiard Table Manufactory,
to a property developer who destroyed it in 1968.

Below: The eastern end of Cheyne Walk, c. 1871, just before the Embankment was built.

Next page: Joy riding outside the Blue Cockatoo, c. 1948.
Even then this was a vintage Renault.

Cheyne Walk—Oakley Street
to the Old Church, c. 1868.

See next page for Hedderley's
view looking east.

CHEYNE WALK

Cheyne Walk, c.1868. Looking east towards Cadogan Pier from the King's Head & Eight Bells.

The Thames Coffee House at the corner of Lawrence Street and Cheyne Walk, c. 1865.

Cheyne Walk looking west from the "King's Head & Eight Bells, c. 1871. The notice in the window on the right reads: "Pale Ale 4d. per pint, Soda & Milk, Guinness & Bitter 2d, Chops & Steaks."

Belle Vue Lodge (91 Cheyne Walk)
and Belle Vue House (92),
the latter reputedly designed by Robert Adam.

The row of houses was built
in the late 18th century on land sold
as building plots by the Moravian Brethren,
then owners of Lindsey House next door,
when they were obliged to raise money
following the death of their leader,
Count Zinzendorff, in 1760.

Elizabeth Cleghorne Stevenson,
later the novelist Mrs Gaskell,
was born at 93 Cheyne Walk in 1810.

The original focus of Chelsea was the Old Church, a place of worship for Sir Thomas More during the 1520's and 30's when he liked to escape the pressures of the Chancellorship and find peace in his riverside home. He added his own chapel to the south aisle in 1528 and his Gothic altar tomb in 1532, three years before his execution by Henry VIII. It is also said that Henry married Jane Seymour here in 1536 prior to the more formal ceremony in Westminster Abbey. She died the following year after giving birth to a son, the future Edward VI. The church More knew may have been built on the site of a Saxon one dating from 789. Certainly the words 'Thelchurche' and 'Chelchurche' occur in papal letters from 1290 and 1299 so there is no doubt that the church is well named. The style of the Old Church we know today is 17th century; at that time a Chelsea artisan enlarged it by tearing down much of the original and re-building in red brick. He spared the More Chapel along with other private chapels and the Renaissance capitals almost certainly designed by Holbein during his visits to More's home.

After a landmine hit the river end of Old Church Street on April 17th, 1941,
there seemed at first to be little hope of the historic parish church of All Saints ever being restored.
The badly battered and roofless More Chapel was barely recognisable.
Yet prompt action enabled 80% of the original tombs, monuments and tablets to be saved.
Within a few weeks the chapel had been cleared of rubble and, with a temporary roof and blacked-out windows,
was back in regular use. By 1958, at a total cost of some £60,000 raised from parishioners
and other well-wishers (a remarkably small sum by present day costs)
the historic church had been completely restored and re-dedicated by the Bishop of London
in the presence of Her Majesty Queen Elizabeth the Queen Mother.

Battersea Bridge seen from a half-way stage in the re-building of the Old Church, c. 1956.

The bomb site in the foreground was still being used by members
of the Chelsea Gardens Guild for individual plots.
It has now been made into the sunken Roper's Garden,
named after Thomas More's son-in-law who married his favourite daughter, Margaret.

Duke Street from the east, looking towards Beaufort Street.

Duke Street, the continuation of Lombard Street from Danvers Street to Beaufort Street,
was named after George Villiers, 1st Duke of Buckingham, who lived for a time in Beaufort House.
As with Lombard Street, the whole south side, including the celebrated Adam and Eve tavern,
came down to allow for the building of the Embankment in the early 1870's.
The north side, notable for a tobacco shop used regularly by Carlyle, lasted until 1889.

Duke Street from the west.

The oldest building in Lombard Street, which ran from the Old Church to Danvers Street, was Arch House, built in the 16th century and occupied by Richard Fletcher, Bishop of London and his dramatist son, John. The thoroughfare that ran underneath the arch was only wide enough for one vehicle, priority going to the first comer. Tradition has it that the Prince Consort was obliged to wait his turn while a tradesman's cart rattled slowly towards him. In the 18th and 19th centuries, the house was divided up inside and painted with publicity slogans outside before its final demolition (along with the whole south side of Lombard Street) to make way for the Embankment, c. 1873. Another local landmark was the Rising Sun tavern, one of Chelsea's best established drinking houses. The other buildings were mainly early 19th century.

Lombard Street and Arch House, c. 1865.

Old Church Street. The Black Lion was one
of Chelsea's oldest inns dating from the late 17th
century, as corroborated by the nearby pump
which was inscribed 1691. The original tavern
was a picturesque wooden building complete
with its own tea gardens and bowling green.

By 1892 it had been modernised,
much to the regret of Chelsea historian
Alfred Beaver, who wrote: "to compare
this quaint old structure with its successor
is to see at a glance what we are losing
in this vast city of ours by the gradual
purposeless destruction of all
that is delightful to the eye", sentiments
that seem even more appropriate today.

A cutting from a 1839 newspaper.

THE "BLACK LION, CHELSEA."

The above house is located in Church Street, and
boasts of a brick and mortar man Y'clept Davis for the
master. Here Sir John Moore formerly blew his cloud
and quaffed the unadulterated beverage composed of
malt and hops. We tumbled in the parlour last Tuesday
last and we found a few choice singing boys. Dick Hack
in the chair, and Newman, the butcher, deputy, Dick
broke wind by singing the "Gipsey Girl." Newman
(whose face bespoke his having swallowed a bottle of
blackstrap daily), came out with "May we ne'er want a
friend or a bottle to give him," in a masterly style
The next was Bob Maynard, who obliged with the
"Battle of the Nile," his voice appeared to be a little
husky, which way be accounted for it by his having go
spliced lately. We advise him not to be so violent in
his next attempt, being fearful he may injure himself
and leave his better half a mourning widow. The little
carpenter was the next called upon but being short Hack,
proposed that a ten gallon cask should be placed on his
chair to enable him to be seen, which was granted, but
in the second verse of "All's Well," the hoops gave
way when down came the little man; no bones were
broken but his brandy hat was shifted and his nob
slightly damaged. The cocky blade after having pulled
himself together, muttered something about the cross
of St. Paul's, which to us was unintelligible. In this
room there are the portraits of the club, not painted by
Sir Thomas Lawrence. We promised to pay them
another visit, shook the landlord by the daddles and
departed to Dulce Donum much entertained.

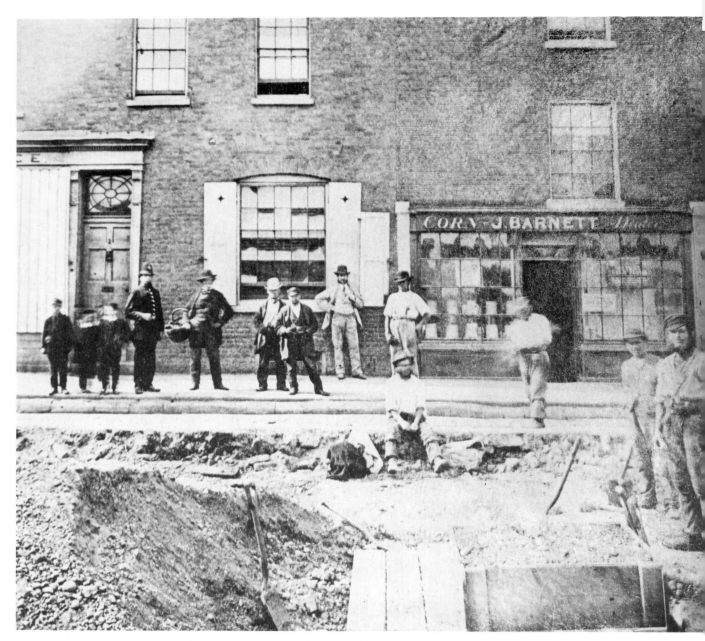

The north side of Duke Street in 1873, taken from the river side
with the hole left by the demolition of the south side in the foreground.

Crosby Hall, moved stone by stone from Bishopsgate in 1908, and re-erected on the site of Duke Street.

After the completion of the Embankment, the remaining side of Lombard Street was gradually modernised. The famous fish shop, patronised by Jane Carlyle, was replaced by C. R. Ashbee's 'art nouveau' house at 74 Cheyne Walk. This was to be Whistler's last Chelsea home; he moved in after the death of his wife, Beatrix, in 1896. This distinctive building, with its beaten copper door, was part of a demolition and redevelopment process that was not completed until 1927. By then the only four old houses that remained were the ones at the Old Church end. The owner of two of them, Major Cyril Sloane Stanley, announced his plans for their replacement with luxury pseudo-Georgian residences, a move that resulted in one of the newly-formed Chelsea Society's first petitions of protest. It was not successful and the destruction continued unabated. The whole row of houses, now a part of Cheyne Walk but known as Lombard Terrace, was destroyed in 1941 on the night the Old Church was hit.

Above left: Lombard Terrace which replaced the north side of Lombard Street.

Below left: 72-77 Cheyne Walk, after the demolition of Arch House and the south side of Lombard Street.

This photograph
was taken by
James Hedderley
(c. 1870)
from the tower
of Chelsea Old Church.
Compare it with
the photographs on
the following pages.
In the background,
the trees surrounding
Cremorne House.

On the left, part of
the old wooden
Battersea Bridge.
See also p.94.

Cremorne House, then known as Chelsea Farm, was built in 1740 by
the Earl of Huntingdon but it owed its final elegance to Viscount Cremorne
who bought it in 1778 and enlarged and embellished it under James Wyatt.
After his death, his American wife, Philadelphia, the great granddaughter
of William Penn, lived there for a further thirteen years,
gaining great popularity by patronising Chelsea tradesmen, something
that was rare at the time. In 1831 Charles Random de Berenger,
Baron de Beaufain a Prussian nobleman, opened The Stadium
"a National Club for the Cultivation of various skilful and manly
exercises" in the grounds. Ten years later the house became the focal point
of Cremorne Pleasure Gardens, until their closure in 1877,
following vociferous local complaints of disorderliness.

View from Chelsea Old Church tower over a century later. (See Page 84).

River front looking east from
Old Battersea Bridge, c. 1870.

The Adam and Eve, a favourite subject
for Walter Greaves, was a quaint
17th century inn with wooden piers
supporting its balconies.
Inside several of the rooms had the walls
hung with fowling-pieces,
relics of the days when Chelsea
was famous for its shooting.
The pub was pulled down in the 1870's
to make way for the building of the
Embankment, but not before it served as
the headquarters for the water sports
at Chelsea's last traditional regatta in 1871.

From the Greaves boatyard, c. 1865.

Two views of the Battersea shore

Battersea Church seen from Lots Road, c. 1965.

The foundation of the Chelsea Steamboat Company
in the late 1830's triggered the building
of Old Cadogan Pier as the headquarters
for their fleet of four small wooden boats.
The pier was completed by 1841
and stood for over 30 years.

When it was demolished, its replacement
was repositioned slightly farther east to allow
more leeway for the newly opened Albert Bridge.

Albert Bridge during its construction in 1873. Opened in September that year, it was
Chelsea's last toll bridge. Its designer, Rowland Mason Ordish, used his straight chain
suspension system, first employed in the Franz Josef Bridge in Prague in 1868.
It is generally agreed that Albert Bridge is the most beautiful of the Thames bridges
but the Ordish method, never highly regarded by engineers, may be responsible for the fact
that it has been the most threatened. Only its temporary closure in the early 1970's
and the addition of a central support have made it safe for modern traffic.
Through the left hand arch can just be seen the old wooden Battersea Bridge
built in 1771 by Earl Spencer who was empowered by Act of Parliament to replace his ferry service.
The bridge was opened to foot passengers in 1773 and to carriage traffic in 1779,
toll charges being ½d. and 4d. respectively. As the bridge cost £15,662,
the Earl must have waited a long time for a return on his investment.
In 1799 it became the first bridge to be lighted at night, with oil lamps along one side;
these were changed to gas in 1824. In 1885 it was pulled down because it was dangerous
but not before it had been immortalised in paintings by Whistler and Greaves.

bert bridge
low tide,
49

Next page: A view of Albert Bridge as it was before the 1951 Festival of Britain
when it was lit up for the first time. In the background, the now demolished Pier Hotel.

The first Chelsea Bridge, built by Thomas Page for the
Commissioners of Woods and Forests and opened in 1858.

It occupies an early fording point, the site of a battle
between the invading Romans and the Britons.
The clash took place in mid stream on the uneven river bed
with the Romans coming out on top—but only, tradition has it,
after they had deployed an elephant which lumbered out of the Battersea woods
to terrify and rout the astounded natives. During excavations for the foundations
of the bridge, skulls and weapons, both bronze and iron, were discovered,
including a beautiful Celtic shield which can be seen in the British Museum.

To the extreme left is the Lister Institute, recently converted into a private
hospital.

Right: The present Chelsea Bridge, built by the London County Council,
which replaced the old suspension bridge in 1936.

Three faces of the World's End pub, still standing today on the site of the ancient wooden tavern referred to in Congreve's *Love for Love*. In Charles II's time, its tea gardens and grounds were favourite haunts of Thames trippers who disembarked and walked up Hob Lane to reach it.

WORLD'S END 1966-1978

Two composite pictures of World's End photographed from the same roof on the north side of King's Road, but twelve years apart. During this interval, the controversial Kensington and Chelsea Council development has taken place. Although the old streets were dingy and the properties largely neglected, the whole neighbourhood was on a human scale, a factor which seems to have been lost. Perhaps the most acceptable feature of the whole scheme is the new purpose-built Community Centre seen on the left of the piazza in the lower picture.

Sporting Chelsea lives on, its name echoed the world over through the Chelsea Football Club. Stamford Bridge was first dreamed of in 1896 by H. E. Mears who, by 1905, had his team officially recognised and entered in the Football League of the day. With £3,000 in the bank, he launched into their first ever League match against West Bromwich Albion. In the same year, 60,000 fans flocked to watch them play against the—even then—mighty Manchester United. By 1906-7 Chelsea had reached the First Division. Nowadays the vast new stadium has banished the once cosy relationship between fans and management but the Saturday afternoon roar still rends the air whenever a goal is scored.

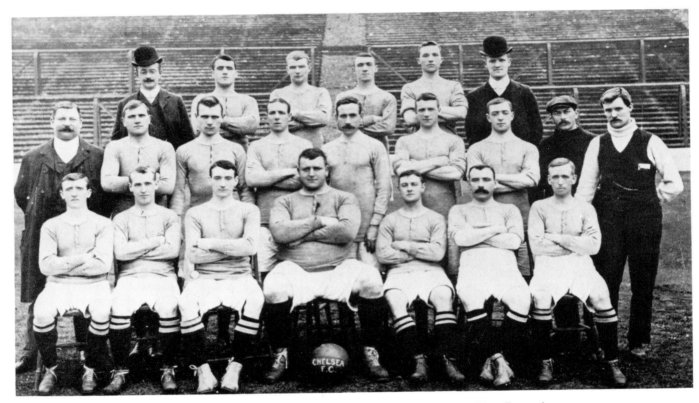

The first Chelsea team-group (1905). Back row: F. W. Parker (hon. fin. sec.), Miller, Donaghy, O'Hara, Craigie, J. T. Robertson (man.). Centre: H. A. Mears (dir.), Watson, Byrne, Mackie, McRoberts, McEwan, Wolff, Randsom and Miller (trainers). Front row: Moran, Key, Robertson, Foulke (capt.), Windridge, Copeland, Kirwan.

The Carlyle Cycling Club has enjoyed a long run of fame. Started by Doctors Redmond and Gunton, it held meetings in Gertrude Street, later transferring to the Six Bells, King's Road. Until 1900, it was an all-male affair; originally members were drawn from the local constables at the Old Chelsea Police Station.

An early meeting of the Cycling Club with Doctors Redmond and Gunton, wearing top hats, seated in the middle.

The Duke of York's Headquarters has seen much sporting history in the making. It was here that the lonely and, at that time unknown, figures of Roger Bannister and Christopher Chataway prepared for Bannister's historic four-minute mile and subsequent honours. Prince Charles had his first lessons in sport in the grounds while at Hill House School, and the Army regularly trained its tug-of-war teams by harnessing them to the unbending plane trees.

As for cricket, it has featured on the Chelsea scene since the days of the Princes club. Founded by James and George Prince, it was situated on and around Lennox Gardens and was the one time headquarters of the M.C.C. Matches were played against an Australian team during their second ever tour of England many years before the Ashes were introduced. Nowadays first class amateur matches can be seen on summer weekends at Burton Court, home ground of the Household Brigade Cricket Club. It is not unusual to see international players, Dexter and Cowdray among them in recent years, playing in scratch sides.

An early print of The Stadium, the sporting club opened by Baron de Beaufain in 1831 in the grounds of Cremorne House.

Many a straight bat as school girls carry on the traditional cricketing and sporting pursuits
at the Duke of York's Headquarters. c. 1957.

The Duke of York's Headquarters was built on the site of Chelsea House, the 18th century residence of the Cadogan family. It was named after the second son of George III, the Duke of York who laid the foundation stone in 1801. At that time he was commander-in-chief of the Army, a position he lost in 1809 when he was disgraced for helping his mistress, Mary Ann Clark, to sell commissions. The building was used as a school for soldier's children until 1909. Girls were allowed until 1823 when it became boys only.

Consecration of new colours presented by The Duke and Duchess of York, June 1897.

Four masters at the school.

The school tuck shop.

The infirmary, c. 1897, which was severely damaged by enemy action during World War II.

Right: A tired Pensioner refreshing himself in the old canteen,
next door to the infirmary and also severely damaged during the war.

Next page: The Royal Hospital tavern on the corner of Franklin's Row provided further opportunities for drinking for pensioners and others. Franklin's Row was named after the enterprising farmer-turned-builder, Thomas Franklin, who put up the first four houses and a pub in 1699. His prosperity was based on his work on the road round three sides of Burton's Court which allowed the original track along the northern facade of the Royal Hospital to be cut off, so completing Sir Christopher Wren's grand design for an impressive approach.

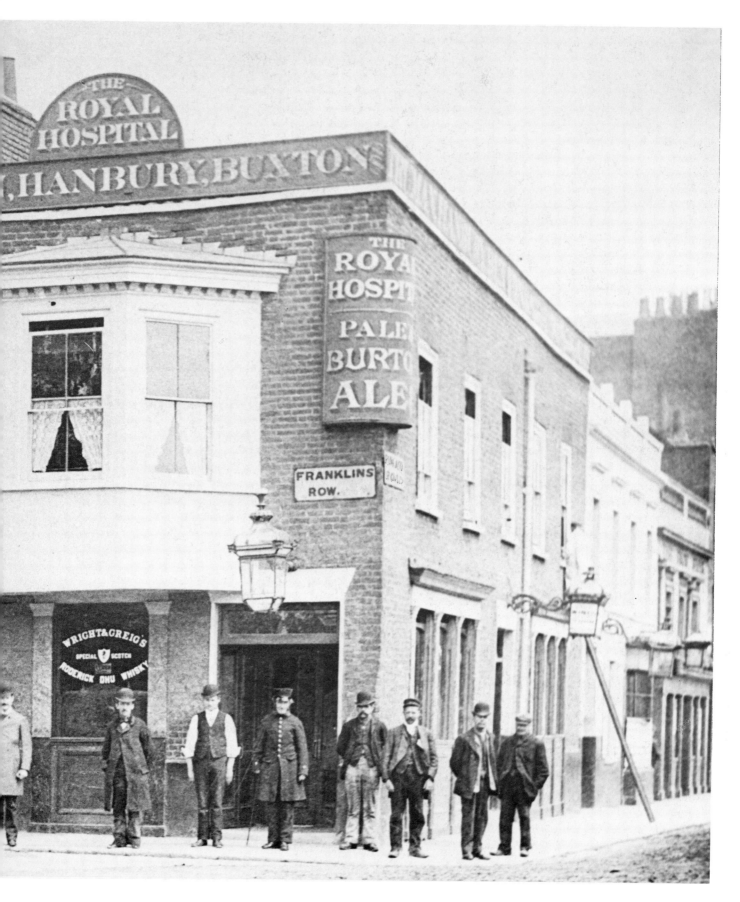

The first Royal Horticultural Society show, held in 1888 in Inner Temple Gardens, was a small affair compared with the five day gardener's paradise we know today. Nevertheless it rapidly became a popular annual event, to the extent that a larger site was urgently needed by 1910. In 1912 The Royal Hospital grounds were chosen for the Royal International Exhibition which was attended by nearly 200,000 visitors. Exhibits from America, Holland, France, Germany and Japan set the cosmopolitan tone that has been a feature of the show ever since. After this success, the Chelsea venue was the automatic choice for subsequent R.H.S. shows.

After four years the show was discontinued for the duration of World War I, starting up again in 1919 and expanding into Ranelagh Gardens in 1922. It became firmly established as part of the social calendar in the 1920's, with neighbouring Chelseans holding tea parties for country acquaintances. The Private View was introduced in 1932 though its privacy was questionable with 15,000 guests causing traffic jams back to Piccadilly.

Following an eight year break, the show was revived in 1947 and it has been going from strength to strength ever since. In the 1970's the emphasis has been on conservation and science in tune with current preoccupations with the environment. Nowadays the Great Marquee covers 3½ acres with rock and water gardens outside, requiring a staff of 2,000 to administer the exhibits and stands alone.

Queen Alexandra at the Royal Chelsea Flower Show in 1913. She was the first in a long line of royal supporters that continues to-day.

Tradition still rules.
Top hats for stewards
(above) and bowlers for
judges *(below)*.

The Mayor, Miss Katherine Acland welcoming H.M. Queen Elizabeth II to the Show in 1959.

A free show maybe, but the Pensioners have seen it all before!

The 142 foot tower is the most striking feature of James Savage's Gothic revival church started in 1820 and consecrated on October 18th, 1824. Built of Bath stone at a cost of £30,000, it replaced the Old Church near the river as the parish church for Chelsea.

Top right: Ben Greet's Company of Shakespearean Players performed
Twelfth Night in the Rectory Gardens, c. 1921.

Bottom right: The Rectory, a substantial Georgian building
set in two acres of garden, by far the largest private estate in Chelsea,
surrounded by a brick wall partly dating from the 17th century.
The garden features a celebrated mulberry tree, allegedly planted by Queen Elizabeth I.

Whistler's association with Chelsea Reach began in 1863 when he rented 7 Lindsey Row (101 Cheyne Walk), two doors down from the Greaves' family home (103). He moved into part of Lindsey House itself (96 Cheyne Walk) in 1866 and lived there for twelve years before going briefly to the uncompleted White House in Tite Street in 1879. Earlier in the century (1808-1824) the famous Victorian engineer, Isambard Kingdom Brunel, designer of the first regular transatlantic steamship, the Great Western, spent much of his childhood in the middle section of Lindsey House (98 Cheyne Walk).

Walter Greaves with William Marchant and Greaves' portrait of Whistler, c. 1904.

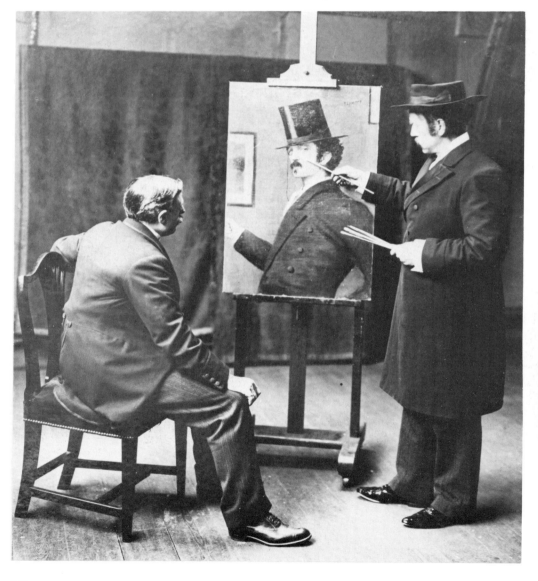

Lindsey House and, to the left, the Greaves boatyard, c.1870.

Left: Portrait of J. M. W. Turner, while painting his picture 'Mercury and Argos', by Charles Turner.

Right: Lindsey Row and the Greaves boatyard. c. 1870.

Below: 6 Davis Place (119 Cheyne Walk), c.1900, where Turner spent the last six years of his life disguised as Mr Booth, the gentleman lodger of Margate landlady, Mrs Booth, who acquired the lease in 1846. The house is next to the Aquatic tavern. Turner died overlooking Chelsea Reach in 1851.

Don Saltero's Tavern (18 Cheyne Walk) on the site of the famous Coffee House
established in 1695 by James Salter, tooth-drawer, barber and antiquarian
as well as ex-travelling head valet to Sir Hans Sloane. His museum of curiosities,
assembled on these journeys, and his Chelsey Super Punch attracted such 'literati'
as Swift, Addison and Smollett and such distinguished visitors as Benjamin Franklin.
The Tavern was demolished in 1867.

A Rossetti family portrait taken by Lewis Carroll in the garden of 16 Cheyne Walk in 1863.
Left to right: Dante Gabriel, Christina, Mrs Rossetti and William Michael.
Dante Gabriel Rossetti lived and worked in the house for over 20 years. See p.56.

Sir Jacob Epstein as a young man in his studio in Lombard Terrace in 1907.

The massive Epstein sculpture, *Jacob Struggling with the Angel*, is moved laboriously into position in the Tate Gallery shortly after the artist's death in 1959.

James Proudfoot contemplates his latest painting while his wife, Ellen Pollock, rehearses Shaw's *Dark Lady of the Sonnets* in the garden at Trafalgar Studios, with Derek Shaw, Joan Heal and Griffith Jones in 1961.

Anthony Gray sculpting the head of Nubar Gulbenkian in Stamford Bridge Studios, c. 1960.

Left: Daniel's Brewery Stores, opposite the old Chelsea Library, in 1896.

Below left: Wentworth Villa, on the same side of Manresa Road, in 1896.
Then a private house owned by a Mr John Brass, it was later divided into studios.
In the background, Trafalgar Studios, a studio block occupied, until its
demolition in 1962, by Stanley Grimm, Mervyn Peake, James Proudfoot,
Ellen Pollock, George Leech and John Bignell, compiler of this book.

Below: Dr Agatha Bowley, consultant psychologist at the Centre for Spastic Children,
Cheyne Walk, sketching the remains of Wentworth Studios before they were pulled down in 1961.
Actress Joan Greenwood lived here during her childhood.

Tradition has it, almost certainly incorrectly, that Charles II had a hunting lodge on the site of The Pheasantry but in fact the nam first appeared in connection with the breeding of pheasants during the mid nineteenth century.

The original house, like the better known Box Farm next door, was early 19th century stucco. Amedée Joubert, a Roy immigrant from France in the 1830's moved his cabinet making and interior decorating business there from Percy Street in 188 adding a facade of red brick and 'dressed stone', together with wrought iron balconies in the style of Louis XV.

The next landmark came in 1916 when Princess Serafina Astafieva, a great niece of Leo Tolstoy and a graduate of the Imperi School of Ballet, took over the building and opened her Russian Dancing Academy. Her star pupils were Anton Dolin, Alic Marks (Markova) and Peggy Hookham (Margot Fonteyn) while her guests included her guide and mentor, Diaghilev, who company she had joined in 1909 for its inaugural trip to Paris.

In 1932 the basement of The Pheasantry (where the Academy had been) was turned into a club under the management of Rer de Meo. Under the initial influence of Augustus John and later of Pietro Annigoni, it became a favourite haunt of artists, writer actors and politicians, its unusual bistro atmosphere and good food at reasonable prices proving a great attraction.

Among the regular post war patrons were Gregory Peck, Aneurin Bevan, Jennie Lee, Francis Bacon and Peter Ustinov. Th house specialities were Shaslik, huge kebabs lighted and served on swords and, naturally, roast pheasant. The club survived Rer de Meo's death in 1958 but closed in 1966 shortly after his partner, Mario Cazzini, died.

Below: Dame Margot Fonteyn and Dame Adeline Genet, President of the Royal Academy of Ballet from 1920-1954.

The Pheasantry before the surrounding buildings were demolished.

The last of the great New Year's Eve Arts Balls, held in 1958/9 at the Royal Albert Hall.
Organised by the prestigious Chelsea Arts Club, the balls were held annually,
first in Chelsea and later in the Albert Hall, from 1908. Every year the decor was designed
by a well known artist, among them Augustus John, Alfred Munnings and Charles Wheeler.
In the late 1950's serious disruptions resulted in the balls being stopped.

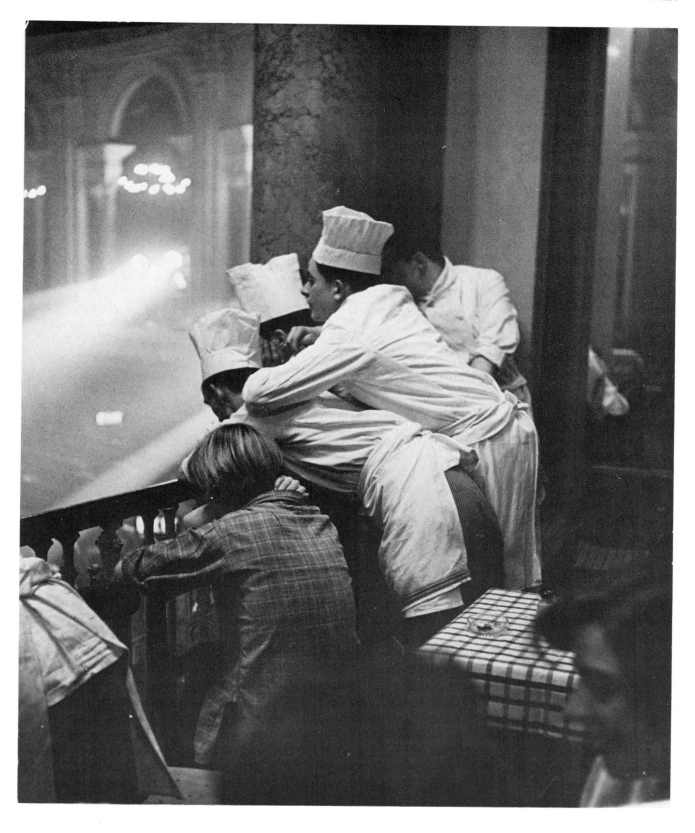

Chefs' view of the festivities below.

Some of the chorus line in Clarkson Rose's show "Twinkle" in 1954.

Left: Chelsea's celebrated variety house, built on the site of the Wilkinson Sword factory in 1902.
In the heyday of music hall, Georgie Wood, George Robey, Sir Harry Lauder, Vesta Tilley, Little Tich
and Gracie Fields were among the entertainers who appeared there. A Chelsea resident recalls elephants
having their toe nails gilded by Indian attendants as they waited in Sydney Street to go on stage
in one of the between-the wars Christmas pantomimes. After 1945 the 'Palace' gradually went down hill,
the victim of the cinema and, especially, television so it was ironic, if hardly surprising,
that it was bought by Granada in 1957 and used as studios until its demolition in the early 1960's.

Right: A Paul Raymond show at the Palace in 1956, just before it was turned into television studios.

Below: Autumn scene outside Chelsea Palace in 1954.

Thirty years ago Chelsea was a popular location for period films
until the replacement of the traditional street lamps with modern ones
destroyed the authenticity.

Left: Scenes in Upper Cheyne Row during the filming of
Around the World in Eighty Days in 1958.

Below: A more modern film in progress under Battersea Bridge.

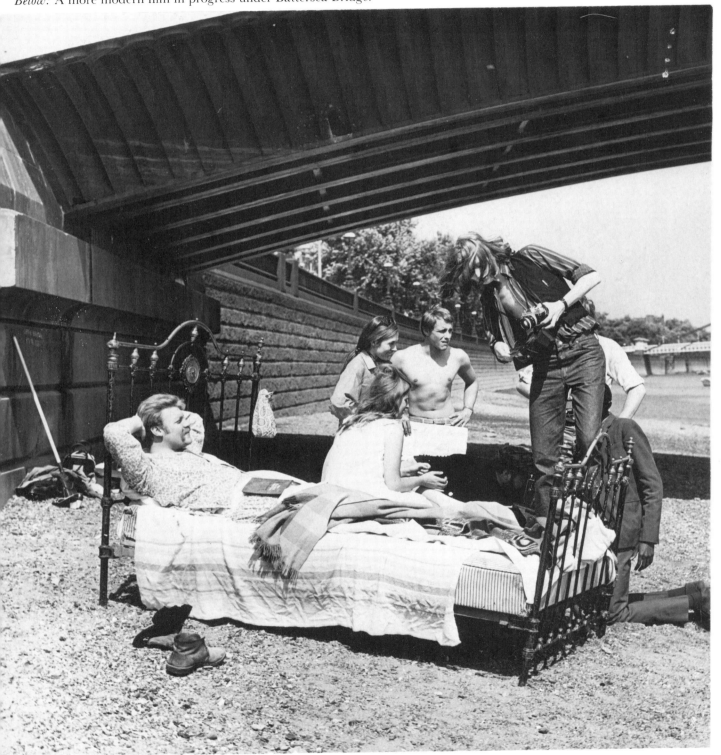

The King's dinner to the poor of Chelsea was held in Burton's Court to celebrate the coronation of Edward VII on July 5th, 1902. 8,000 guests were invited, each to bring his own knife and fork. The Times correspondent described it as a "fiasco" and continued his report: "At two o'clock the crowd of people, exceeding by some thousands those who had a right to be present, rushed in. Children who had no business to be present were there in large numbers, and sturdy roughs and women with babies at the breast. Personally I effected an entrance with extreme difficulty and my eyes fell at once upon a horrid scene. Scores of people were wandering to and from in loud complaining, the stewards were reduced to ladling out tinned beef—which the poor are known to abominate—out of baskets with their bare hands, some guests were stuffing handfuls of pudding and stray viands into their pockets and then asking for more, puddings and cakes were stated to be mouldy, and discontent was universal. The most odious accusations were made, sometimes in the foulest language, against the ladies who had volunteered to help: the supply of beer ran short and finally rather than face an infuriated table with the announcement that there was no beer left and no tobacco, my friend left the grounds and came to my house, dirty and exhausted."

Meanwhile 200 of Chelsea's domestic servants, all of them connected with the Metropolitan Association for Befriending Young Servants, celebrated the coronation more happily in the Assembly Room of the Town Hall. There they sat at six large tables "prettily decorated with flowers and bearing an abundance of luxurious fare including cake and bread and butter, strawberries, cherries and tarts". They were waited on by thirty to forty ladies and entertained after tea with music and singing. Before they left at 6 o'clock, they were given brooches from the Queen Alexandra and gifts from Lady Cadogan.

The oldest sporting event in the rowing world is the Doggett's Annual Coat and Badge race. It was started by Thomas Doggett, comedian and manager of Drury Lane, in 1715 to mark the accession of George I. The race took place between London Bridge and Chelsea, a distance of four miles, five furlongs, a contest between waterman's apprentices in light boats rowing against the tide.

Left: An early Victorian print of the race.

Below left: The Old Swan Tavern, the finishing line
in Victorian times. It was a victim of the Embankment
in the 1870's but it is commemorated today by Old Swan House,
designed by Norman Shaw.

Below: An unusually early industrial photograph by James Hedderley,
c. 1865. Viger's timber yard on the western border of Chelsea.

Disappearing Dairies
Almost the last of the horse-drawn vehicles on the streets were the milkman's vans. As the numerous independent dairies were swallowed up by the Coop, United and Express Dairies, so the ponies disappeared too.

Left: Interior of Wright's Dairies.
Right: Dolly and Daisie.
Below right: Nobby outside Trafalgar Studios, Manresa Road, c. 1958.

Below: Francis' Dairy originated in Wellington Street before moving to King's Road.

S. Margrie, great grandfather of the present owner, started his farrier's business in Flood Street
in 1864, transferring to Arthur Street in 1880. The family remained in the same premises
until the terrace was demolished c.1960. Over the years the farrier's trade diminished with the
disappearance of horse traffic, but E. E. Margrie, grandson of the founder,
adapted to the changing times and became well known to many Chelsea artists as a maker of
armatures for sculptors.

After seven years in premises behind the Pier Hotel in Cheyne Walk,
the family business now flourishes in Fulham Palace Road.

Interior of the Dovehouse Street Forge c. 1950.

Camera Square was built in the 1820's. Its terraces of small houses were replaced some hundred years later by the present well-designed area known as Chelsea Park Gardens.

Right: a young lady with birdcage in Camera Square, c.1895

Below: corner shop before inflation. This is probably the site of the houses, built in 1920, where Sir Alfred Munnings lived until his death in 1959.

Peter Jones, Sloane Square. The old building was decorated and beflagged on 4 October 1900 to celebrate a Chelsea Festival.

The Fashion Salon, complete with potted palms and sinister headless dummies.

David Rawnsley, a former art director in the Rank Film Studios, in 1952 took over the lease of Buchanan's old workshop in Radnor Walk (where hand-pushed milk floats had been built for nearly a century). Here he established the modern Chelsea Pottery and the Rawnsley Academy to produce high quality "art" decorated ceramics for collectors all over the world. He quickly established a high reputation and opened further academies in the West Indies and Capri. Since Rawnsley died in 1977 the Chelsea Pottery has been successfully continued by Brian Hubbard (*seen below*).

The earlier mid-eighteenth century Chelsea China factory lay behind the west side of Lawrence Street. Although its precise location is not certain, large quantities of broken porcelain biscuit have recently been dug up in the garden behind no. 15.

Before concluding this section on Trade and Industry, Chelsea's centuries-old connection with dairy farming, horticulture, fruit- and market-gardening must be stressed. Only the low-lying swamps of what we now call Belgravia and Pimlico separated the teeming cities of London and Westminster from the fertile fields of Chelsea, little more than an hour away on foot.

Even in the last quarter of the nineteenth century, when Hedderley was recording many of the scenes in this book, relics of these activities were still visible within yards of the King's and Fulham Roads. Cows were milked daily by the last owner of Box Farm, Mr Pulham Markham Evans, where Markham's Street and Square now lie. He may, too, have been related to another Evans' farm, better known as Chelsea Farm, part of the Cremorne Estate to the west of World's End.

Box Farm was to go in 1900, leaving the Pheasantry for studios and, in the basement, a successful club and restaurant flourished until about twenty years ago when it was rebuilt retaining the old façade and pretentious triumphal arch.

Many leaseholders held grazing rights on Chelsea Common, which covered several hundred acres north of King's Road from Knightsbridge to Stamford Bridge but is now sadly reduced to a tiny triangle at the junction of Elystan, Cale and Markham Streets.

Kip's View of the Beaufort Estate on the ensuing pages gives a vivid idea of the extent of Chelsea's "cultured lands, sacred to Flora . . ."

This charming blonde graced the corner of Glebe Place and King's Road.

Sadly, even the itinerant flower sellers seem to have moved away.
After a lifetime of flower-selling in the King's Road, this familiar character disappeared in the late sixties driven out, perhaps, by increasing traffic.

Kip's well-known view of the Beaufort Estate in Chelsea (see pp. 156-7) was drawn about 1689. The Beaufort House was originally built for Thomas More in 1524. It passed through many different hands after More's execution in 1535, until in 1681 it was bought by the first Duke of Beaufort for £5000. After the death of the Dowager Duchess of Beaufort in 1716, it remained empty and neglected until Sir Hans Sloane bought it in 1737 in a sadly delapidated condition. Three years later he ordered that this historic house be demolished.

Moravian Close

By an ironic quirk of fate barely ten years later Count Zinzendorf, a wealthy Bohemian landlord who championed a small protestant group from Moravia (part of modern Czechoslovakia), came to Chelsea looking for a suitable house with land to form a settlement for the refugees. He bought Lindsey house "together with all the land up to Kings Road". He was licensed by the Archbishop of Canterbury to be the first bishop of the brethren in England. Unfortunately he died very soon afterwards and plans for the settlement had to be abandoned for lack of money. Lindsey house and much of the land was sold, but they managed to retain a plot of almost two acres where they had already built their church and a manse for their minister. Both were substantially built upon the solid stone foundations laid down more than two centuries earlier to support Sir Thomas More's stables. During his lifetime, no doubt, More would have condemned these Moravian Brethren as heretics. Yet, if he ever looks down upon his former Chelsea home, he might well nod with approval at the persistence of their simple faith and brotherly way of life – qualities, indeed, which were advocated in his own *Utopia*.

The church is still used for regular worship though a large part of the building has been divided up into artist studios. The former stable yard, more than one acre in extent, has been the consecrated burial ground for over 400 of the faithful ever since their original settlement here, and is still in occasional use.

Kip's View, *c.*1689 (*overleaf*)
Table of reference (pp. 156-7)

1. The King's Road
2. Fulham Road
3. Church Lane (now Old Church Street)
4. Milman Street
5. Paulton Sq. (approx.)
C. Chelsea Common
6. Beaufort House (Thos. More's)
7. More's stables
8. More's stable yard
9. Lindsey House
B . . . B Beaufort St. to Battersea Bridge

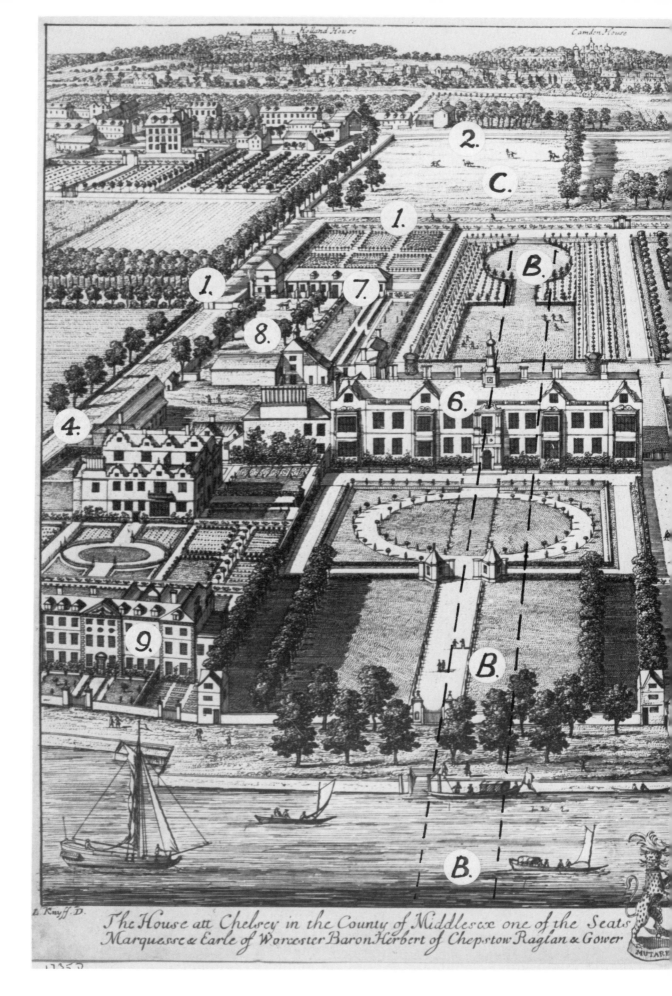

The House att Chelsey in the County of Middlesex one of the Seats
Marquesse & Earle of Worcester Baron Herbert of Chepstow Raglan & Gower

Kensington House

C.

1.

3.

3.

5.

of the Most Noble & Potent Prince Henry Duke of Beaufort
and Knight of the Most Noble order of the Garter.

I. Kyp Sc

13

Above: The Moravian Church and Manse, built in 1753, upon the original stone foundation of Thomas More's stables. (See Kip's View pp. 156-7.)

Below: There are no contemporary records of what More's house actually looked like. This was drawn in 1891 by Alfred Beaver, probably based on Kip's drawing.

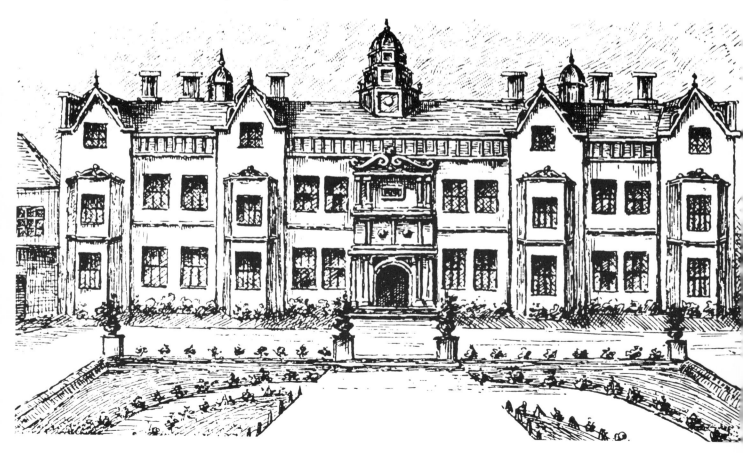

In the Year of Our
Lord 1524

Sir Thomas More
bought land here and
afterwards built the
Great House

1535 Confiscated by
King Henry VIII at
the time of More's
attainder

1536 Granted to the
1st Marquis of
Winchester

1575 Assigned to the
Lord and Lady Dacre
of the South

1595 Bequeathed to
Lord Burleigh

1597 New fronted by
Sir Robert Cecil

1599 Conveyed to the
Earl of Lincoln

1615 Inherited by Sir
Arthur Gorges and
Dame Elizabeth his
wife

1619 Bought by the
Earl of Middlesex

1625 Forfeited to
King Charles I

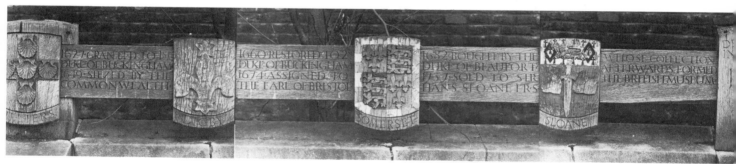

1627 Granted to the
1st Duke of
Buckingham

1660 Restored to the
2nd Duke of
Buckingham

1674 Assigned to the
Earl of Bristol

1682 Bought by the
Duke of Beaufort

whose collection
afterwards formed the
British Museum

1649 Seized by the
Commonwealth

1737 Sold to Sir Hans
Sloane F.R.S.

Demolished in the year
1740

Parallel with the south wall of the Moravian Burial Ground is a long stone bench with carved wood coats of arms of all
the occupiers of More's Great House (1524) until Sir Hans Sloane demolished it in 1740. It was designed and executed
in the present studio here by Ernest Gillick ARA and his wife. Later, it was Mrs Gillick who designed the coinage with
the present Queen's head.

After reading the inscriptions, one American visitor exclaimed, "why, my goodness! You have the whole of England's
history right here!" A slight exaggeration – but it certainly covers a momentous two hundred years.

ACKNOWLEDGEMENTS

Books and authorities consulted include: Alfred Beaver *Memorials of Old Chelsea;* Ursula Bloom *Rosemary for Chelsea;* Richards Edmonds *From the Five Fields to the World's End;* William Gaunt *Chelsea;* Thea Holme *Chelsea;* Nesta Macdonald *The History of the Pheasantry Chelsea 1766-1977;* Hester Marsden-Smedley *The Chelsea Flower Show;* Tom Pocock *Chelsea Reach.*

Thanks are due to the following institutions and individuals for the use of information and photographs: The Kensington and Chelsea Library, The Tate Gallery, John Lewis Partnership Archives, The Library of the Royal Horticultural Society, The Chelsea Society, The G.L.C. Photographic Library, The Marx Memorial Library, The Chelsea Football Club, Lady Epstein, Marit Aschan, Joyce Morgan, Tom Pocock, The Rev. C. E. Leighton Thomson, Dr Patrick Lovett, Faith Sheppard, Hester Marsden-Smedley, Jim Barnard, Lucette de la Fougère, Miss Clisby, E. J. Margrie, Miss Q. R. Francis.

I would especially like to thank Mrs Pratt and the always helpful staff of the local records department at Chelsea library.

Edited by John Bignell
Research by Minty Clinch
Sport captions by Loraine Knowles

ISBN 0-7090-4976-5